D0516538

we are readers

READING IS MAGIC

A Book Log for Families

Foreword by Emma Straub

ABRAMS IMAGE • NEW YORK

"There are perhaps no days of our childhood we lived so fully as those we spent with a favorite book."

MARCEL PROUST

There is no time before reading. As a parent of two small children (three and five years old, at this precise moment), making sure that my children have been surrounded by books since the day they were born is the only thing that I know I've done right. Sleep training, weaning, discipline or lack thereof—who's to say? But putting books in front of their faces and watching their newborn eyes blink with excitement? Reading books over and over, day after day, until we all know them by heart? YES.

This is not my idea. Like so many things about me—my nose, my laugh, my inability to leave a party without saying goodbye to everyone six times—it belonged first to my mother. For twenty-five years, my mother ran a program called Read to Me, which ran workshops with young parents, encouraging them to read to their children with baby books and goofy homemade art projects that were all about getting moms to interact with their children using those most ancient connective tissues—words and pictures.

My mother's work—coupled with my father's work as a novelist, and multiplied by the bookshelves lining every room of the house we lived in—and the pleasure I saw my parents get from books meant that I was all in, from day one. Books were as much of a comfort to me as my special blanket, and now that is true for my children, too. Some families do this with cooking—mine did it with books. It was the thing we did best, the place we came together, and the act that both gave me confidence and offered a respite from everything else. This is still true for me—books are the answer. If I have a problem, or a question, or a desire, I turn to a book.

Here is what this journal can do:

- keep track of the books that your children love
- keep track of the books that make you cry every time you read them (and always will, no matter how old your children get)
- help you figure out what to read next

The recommended reading lists at the end of this journal are compiled from suggestions made by booksellers, authors, and children's book advocates. Organized by theme, these are the books that you'll use as tools to help your children navigate the tricky business of growing up.

And let me reassure you: If you put this journal down for six months, don't feel guilty when you pick it up again. Books don't mind waiting. You're doing a wonderful job.

Emma Straub

Reading as a Family

Reading with Babies and Toddlers

BY SUSAN STRAUB
(Emma Straub's mom)

Babies learn everything through their senses as they see, hear, smell, taste, and touch. Introducing them to the magic of stories and art in books will enhance both of your lives—it's a promise! Once babies start to move, they are ready for more interactive books that are designed for touching, lifting, pulling, and poking. Toddlers may not stay in your lap for long, but they are still listening to the story and will likely rejoin you to touch the bunny's tail or see their favorite page.

☐ *I Kissed the Baby!*
by Mary Murphy / ages 2–3

Here are joyous conversations about interacting with a baby. The refrain is infectious, and you *will* give and get at least one kiss!

☐ *Hug*
by Jez Alborough / ages 2–3

The little gorilla wants and notices hugs galore. You *will* give and get at least one hug!

☐ *Peek-A Who?*
by Nina Laden / ages 0–3

Clever rhymes and illustrations encourage little ones to guess who is peeking through the die-cut windows on the pages.

☐ *Now*
by Antoinette Portis / ages 3–6

A young girl enjoys her favorite breeze, leaf, tree, smell. Her simple joy radiates. Enjoy it *now*.

☐ *More More More,*
Said the Baby
by Vera B. Williams / ages 1–7

These three distinct love stories feature toddlers with a dad, a grandmother, and a mother who adore their little ones. The toddlers want more, more, more.

☐ *Baby Says*
by John Steptoe / ages 2–4

This remarkable board book captures two brothers at play. When the older brother springs the baby from his crib, there are extra visible challenges and delights.

☐ *Mr. Gumpy's Outing*
by John Burningham / ages 4 & up

A delightful "pile-on" book. Mr. Gumpy invites children and animals for a boat ride. Inevitably, the boat tips, and he invites them all for tea.

☐ *May We Have Enough*
to Share
by Richard Van Camp / ages 3 & up

This board book showcases parent-baby photos and reminds us to be grateful for natural love.

☐ *The Monster at the End*
of This Book
by Jon Stone,
ill. by Michael Smollin / ages 3–7

"Don't turn the page," pleads Grover. But we do, and unsurprisingly, we find Grover at the end.

Recommended authors:
Sandra Boynton, Eric Carle, Julie Flett, Gyo Fujikawa, Tad Hills, Helen Oxenbury, Leslie Patricelli, Simms Taback, Denise Fleming, Kevin Henkes, James Marshall, Jan Ormerod, Mo Willems, Nina Crews, Paul Galdone, Leo and Diane Dillon, Rosemary Wells, and Richard Scarry

Reading with Children

BY ANGIE MURCHISON TALLY, the Country Bookshop

1

Dig down deep into your child's interests—dinosaurs, ballet, trains, cats, magic, soccer, anything that excites them. Encourage these interests with both fiction and nonfiction books.

2

Make a trip to your local bookstore or library on a regular basis. You can take your child to story times, author events, and special programs, or plan a regular Saturday afternoon outing. Bookstores and libraries will constantly put the newest and the most popular books on your child's radar.

3

Read together by selecting a book just a bit above your child's personal reading level and read a chapter aloud to them a few times a week.

4

Let kids read for *fun*! While reading programs encourage children to push their reading level, none of us read at our maximum reading level all the time. Old favorites, picture books, and shorter books are absolutely fine for older and more advanced readers.

5

Embrace graphic novels. Kids read these over and over, and you may even usher nonreaders into becoming voracious readers by introducing them to this genre.

Reading with Middle Graders

JESSI BLACKSTOCK, Magers & Quinn Booksellers

1

Teach middle graders how to browse in a bookstore. Focus on one shelf at a time to avoid getting overwhelmed. Encourage kids to pick up books with covers that they like and read the back cover and first paragraph to see if the writing really grabs them.

2

Try not to let a particular series or book become too precious (e.g., the Harry Potter rut). Help your middle grader find new books with similar themes to encourage reading something new. You can ask a bookseller or librarian for help finding titles that are similar to established favorites.

3

Allow middle graders to start and stop books as they wish. If a book doesn't have them hooked, it is going to be a battle to get them to read.

4

Read what your middle grader is reading and create conversations around the book by talking about it casually over dinner or in the car.

5

Keep reading out loud to your middle grader. You can select books that may be too difficult for middle graders to read on their own, or focus on books that are just fun to read together. This will encourage building conversation around books, growing vocabulary, and learning to follow complicated plot structures.

Family Reading Tips

BY JESSI BLACKSTOCK & ANGIE MURCHISON TALLY

Surround your child with books any way you can. Let them see you read and talk about what you are reading. Allow each child a personal bookcase in their bedroom for their favorite cherished titles.

Give children gift certificates to a local bookshop for their birthday or other holidays and let them choose anything they want. Choosing a book of one's own is a powerful thing.

Go on family outings that involve books. Free author events can be really interesting for parents and kids alike. Meeting an author and owning a personalized, autographed book can set a reader on fire for a particular title or series.

Establish a reading hour at home so that everyone, including parents and caregivers, sits down and reads together.

Organize an all-family read once a year. Maybe include extended family (e.g., grandparents and cousins), then choose a book that interests everyone, and read that title over a chosen month. Get together for a themed party at the end of the month to discuss the book!

"There are many little ways to enlarge your child's world. Love of books is the best of all."

JACQUELINE KENNEDY

Reading Tally

Fill in a star each time your child completes a new book. (There are 100 total!)

Favorite Books

Your child's most beloved books, year by year

1
YEAR OLD

_____

_____

_____

2
YEARS OLD

_____

_____

_____

3
YEARS OLD

_____

_____

_____

4 YEARS OLD

_____

_____

_____

5 YEARS OLD

_____

_____

_____

6 YEARS OLD

_____

_____

_____

TIMELINE

Favorite Books

7

YEARS OLD

_____

_____

_____

8

YEARS OLD

_____

_____

_____

9

YEARS OLD

_____

_____

_____

10
YEARS OLD

_____

_____

_____

11
YEARS OLD

_____

_____

_____

12
YEARS OLD

_____

_____

_____

"The love of learning, the sequestered nooks, and all the sweet serenity of books."

HENRY WADSWORTH LONGFELLOW

Parent's Wishlist

A list of books you want to read with your child someday

_____

_____

_____

_____

_____

_____

_____

_____

_____

_____

_____

First, Best, Most

First book I read on my own

_____

_____

Favorite book from childhood

_____

_____

Book I've read over and over

_____

_____

Best book I've read lately

_____

_____

Character I'm most like

_____

_____

Best thing about reading

_____

_____

First, Best, Most

First book I read on my own

_____

_____

Favorite book so far

_____

_____

Book I've read over and over

_____

_____

Best book I've read at school

_____

_____

Character I'm most like

_____

_____

Best thing about reading

_____

_____

What if . . .

If I could meet any character from a book in real life, I would choose . . .

_____

_____

If I could enter the world of any book, it would be . . .

_____

_____

If I could change any book's ending, I would change . . .

_____

_____

If I could ask my favorite author a question, it would be . . .

_____

_____

If I were to write my own book, it would be about . . .

_____

_____

What if . . .

If I could meet any character from a book in real life, I would choose . . .

_____

_____

If I could enter the world of any book, it would be . . .

_____

_____

If I could change any book's ending, I would change . . .

_____

_____

If I could ask my favorite author a question, it would be . . .

_____

_____

If I were to write my own book, it would be about . . .

_____

_____

"The knowledge that a good book awaits one at the end of a day, makes that a better day."

UNKNOWN

Our Favorite Bedtime Books

A list of books that the family has read before bed

_____

_____

_____

_____

_____

_____

_____

_____

_____

_____

_____

Book Log

TITLE:

AUTHOR:

ILLUSTRATOR:

DATE FIRST READ:

WHERE DID WE GET THIS BOOK?

HOW MUCH YOU'VE READ THIS BOOK:

A
LITTLE

A
LOT

HOW DID THIS BOOK MAKE YOU FEEL?

KID RATING:

PARENT RATING:

THINGS TO REMEMBER:

_____

_____

_____

_____

_____

TITLE:

AUTHOR:

ILLUSTRATOR:

DATE FIRST READ:

WHERE DID WE GET THIS BOOK?

HOW MUCH YOU'VE READ THIS BOOK:

A
LITTLE

A
LOT

HOW DID THIS BOOK MAKE YOU FEEL?

KID RATING:

PARENT RATING:

THINGS TO REMEMBER:

_____

_____

_____

_____

_____

TITLE:

AUTHOR:

ILLUSTRATOR:

DATE FIRST READ:

WHERE DID WE GET THIS BOOK?

HOW MUCH YOU'VE READ THIS BOOK:

A
LITTLE

A
LOT

HOW DID THIS BOOK MAKE YOU FEEL?

KID RATING:

PARENT RATING:

THINGS TO REMEMBER:

_____

_____

_____

_____

_____

TITLE:

AUTHOR:

ILLUSTRATOR:

DATE FIRST READ:

WHERE DID WE GET THIS BOOK?

HOW MUCH YOU'VE READ THIS BOOK:

A
LITTLE

A
LOT

HOW DID THIS BOOK MAKE YOU FEEL?

KID RATING:

PARENT RATING:

THINGS TO REMEMBER:

_____

_____

_____

_____

_____

TITLE:

AUTHOR:

ILLUSTRATOR:

DATE FIRST READ:

WHERE DID WE GET THIS BOOK?

HOW MUCH YOU'VE READ THIS BOOK:

A
LITTLE

A
LOT

HOW DID THIS BOOK MAKE YOU FEEL?

KID RATING:

PARENT RATING:

THINGS TO REMEMBER:

_____

_____

_____

_____

_____

TITLE:

AUTHOR:

ILLUSTRATOR:

DATE FIRST READ:

WHERE DID WE GET THIS BOOK?

HOW MUCH YOU'VE READ THIS BOOK:

A
LITTLE

A
LOT

HOW DID THIS BOOK MAKE YOU FEEL?

KID RATING:

PARENT RATING:

THINGS TO REMEMBER:

_____

_____

_____

_____

_____

TITLE:

AUTHOR:

ILLUSTRATOR:

DATE FIRST READ:

WHERE DID WE GET THIS BOOK?

HOW MUCH YOU'VE READ THIS BOOK:

A
LITTLE

A
LOT

HOW DID THIS BOOK MAKE YOU FEEL?

KID RATING:

PARENT RATING:

THINGS TO REMEMBER:

_____

_____

_____

_____

_____

TITLE:

AUTHOR:

ILLUSTRATOR:

DATE FIRST READ:

WHERE DID WE GET THIS BOOK?

HOW MUCH YOU'VE READ THIS BOOK:

A
LITTLE

A
LOT

HOW DID THIS BOOK MAKE YOU FEEL?

KID RATING:

PARENT RATING:

THINGS TO REMEMBER:

_____

_____

_____

_____

_____

TITLE:

AUTHOR:

ILLUSTRATOR:

DATE FIRST READ:

WHERE DID WE GET THIS BOOK?

HOW MUCH YOU'VE READ THIS BOOK:

A LITTLE

A LOT

HOW DID THIS BOOK MAKE YOU FEEL?

KID RATING:

PARENT RATING:

THINGS TO REMEMBER:

_____

_____

_____

_____

_____

"I HAVE ALWAYS IMAGINED THAT PARADISE WILL BE A KIND OF LIBRARY."

JORGE LUIS BORGES

TITLE:

AUTHOR:

ILLUSTRATOR:

DATE FIRST READ:

WHERE DID WE GET THIS BOOK?

HOW MUCH YOU'VE READ THIS BOOK:

A
LITTLE

A
LOT

HOW DID THIS BOOK MAKE YOU FEEL?

KID RATING:

PARENT RATING:

THINGS TO REMEMBER:

_____

_____

_____

_____

TITLE:

AUTHOR:

ILLUSTRATOR:

DATE FIRST READ:

WHERE DID WE GET THIS BOOK?

HOW MUCH YOU'VE READ THIS BOOK:

A
LITTLE

A
LOT

HOW DID THIS BOOK MAKE YOU FEEL?

KID RATING:

PARENT RATING:

THINGS TO REMEMBER:

_____

_____

_____

_____

_____

TITLE:

AUTHOR:

ILLUSTRATOR:

DATE FIRST READ:

WHERE DID WE GET THIS BOOK?

HOW MUCH YOU'VE READ THIS BOOK:

A
LITTLE

A
LOT

HOW DID THIS BOOK MAKE YOU FEEL?

KID RATING:

PARENT RATING:

THINGS TO REMEMBER:

_____

_____

_____

_____

_____

TITLE:

AUTHOR:

ILLUSTRATOR:

DATE FIRST READ:

WHERE DID WE GET THIS BOOK?

HOW MUCH YOU'VE READ THIS BOOK:

A
LITTLE

A
LOT

HOW DID THIS BOOK MAKE YOU FEEL?

KID RATING:

PARENT RATING:

THINGS TO REMEMBER:

_____

_____

_____

_____

_____

TITLE:

AUTHOR:

ILLUSTRATOR:

DATE FIRST READ:

WHERE DID WE GET THIS BOOK?

HOW MUCH YOU'VE READ THIS BOOK:

A
LITTLE

A
LOT

HOW DID THIS BOOK MAKE YOU FEEL?

KID RATING:

PARENT RATING:

THINGS TO REMEMBER:

_____

_____

_____

_____

_____

TITLE:

AUTHOR:

ILLUSTRATOR:

DATE FIRST READ:

WHERE DID WE GET THIS BOOK?

HOW MUCH YOU'VE READ THIS BOOK:

A
LITTLE

A
LOT

HOW DID THIS BOOK MAKE YOU FEEL?

KID RATING:

PARENT RATING:

THINGS TO REMEMBER:

_____

_____

_____

_____

_____

TITLE:

AUTHOR:

ILLUSTRATOR:

DATE FIRST READ:

WHERE DID WE GET THIS BOOK?

HOW MUCH YOU'VE READ THIS BOOK:

A
LITTLE

A
LOT

HOW DID THIS BOOK MAKE YOU FEEL?

KID RATING:

PARENT RATING:

THINGS TO REMEMBER:

_____

_____

_____

_____

_____

TITLE:

AUTHOR:

ILLUSTRATOR:

DATE FIRST READ:

WHERE DID WE GET THIS BOOK?

HOW MUCH YOU'VE READ THIS BOOK:

A
LITTLE

A
LOT

HOW DID THIS BOOK MAKE YOU FEEL?

KID RATING:

PARENT RATING:

THINGS TO REMEMBER:

_____

_____

_____

_____

_____

TITLE:

AUTHOR:

ILLUSTRATOR:

DATE FIRST READ:

WHERE DID WE GET THIS BOOK?

HOW MUCH YOU'VE READ THIS BOOK:

A
LITTLE

A
LOT

HOW DID THIS BOOK MAKE YOU FEEL?

KID RATING:

PARENT RATING:

THINGS TO REMEMBER:

_____

_____

_____

_____

_____

"Let us read and let us dance—two amusements that will never do any harm to the world."

VOLTAIRE

TITLE:

AUTHOR:

ILLUSTRATOR:

DATE FIRST READ:

WHERE DID WE GET THIS BOOK?

HOW MUCH YOU'VE READ THIS BOOK:

A
LITTLE

A
LOT

HOW DID THIS BOOK MAKE YOU FEEL?

KID RATING:

PARENT RATING:

THINGS TO REMEMBER:

_____

_____

_____

_____

_____

TITLE:

AUTHOR:

ILLUSTRATOR:

DATE FIRST READ:

WHERE DID WE GET THIS BOOK?

HOW MUCH YOU'VE READ THIS BOOK:

A
LITTLE

A
LOT

HOW DID THIS BOOK MAKE YOU FEEL?

KID RATING:

PARENT RATING:

THINGS TO REMEMBER:

_____

_____

_____

_____

_____

TITLE:

AUTHOR:

ILLUSTRATOR:

DATE FIRST READ:

WHERE DID WE GET THIS BOOK?

HOW MUCH YOU'VE READ THIS BOOK:

A
LITTLE

A
LOT

HOW DID THIS BOOK MAKE YOU FEEL?

KID RATING:

PARENT RATING:

THINGS TO REMEMBER:

_____

_____

_____

_____

_____

TITLE:

AUTHOR:

ILLUSTRATOR:

DATE FIRST READ:

WHERE DID WE GET THIS BOOK?

HOW MUCH YOU'VE READ THIS BOOK:

A
LITTLE

A
LOT

HOW DID THIS BOOK MAKE YOU FEEL?

KID RATING:

PARENT RATING:

THINGS TO REMEMBER:

_____

_____

_____

_____

_____

TITLE:

AUTHOR:

ILLUSTRATOR:

DATE FIRST READ:

WHERE DID WE GET THIS BOOK?

HOW MUCH YOU'VE READ THIS BOOK:

A
LITTLE

A
LOT

HOW DID THIS BOOK MAKE YOU FEEL?

KID RATING:

PARENT RATING:

THINGS TO REMEMBER:

_____

_____

_____

_____

_____

TITLE:

AUTHOR:

ILLUSTRATOR:

DATE FIRST READ:

WHERE DID WE GET THIS BOOK?

HOW MUCH YOU'VE READ THIS BOOK:

A
LITTLE

A
LOT

HOW DID THIS BOOK MAKE YOU FEEL?

KID RATING:

PARENT RATING:

THINGS TO REMEMBER:

_____

_____

_____

_____

_____

TITLE:

AUTHOR:

ILLUSTRATOR:

DATE FIRST READ:

WHERE DID WE GET THIS BOOK?

HOW MUCH YOU'VE READ THIS BOOK:

A
LITTLE

A
LOT

HOW DID THIS BOOK MAKE YOU FEEL?

KID RATING:

PARENT RATING:

THINGS TO REMEMBER:

_____

_____

_____

_____

TITLE:

AUTHOR:

ILLUSTRATOR:

DATE FIRST READ:

WHERE DID WE GET THIS BOOK?

HOW MUCH YOU'VE READ THIS BOOK:

A
LITTLE

A
LOT

HOW DID THIS BOOK MAKE YOU FEEL?

KID RATING:

PARENT RATING:

THINGS TO REMEMBER:

_____

_____

_____

_____

_____

TITLE:

AUTHOR:

ILLUSTRATOR:

DATE FIRST READ:

WHERE DID WE GET THIS BOOK?

HOW MUCH YOU'VE READ THIS BOOK:

A
LITTLE

A
LOT

HOW DID THIS BOOK MAKE YOU FEEL?

KID RATING:

PARENT RATING:

THINGS TO REMEMBER:

_____

_____

_____

_____

_____

"TODAY A READER, TOMORROW A LEADER."

W. FUSSELMAN

TITLE:

AUTHOR:

ILLUSTRATOR:

DATE FIRST READ:

WHERE DID WE GET THIS BOOK?

HOW MUCH YOU'VE READ THIS BOOK:

A
LITTLE

A
LOT

HOW DID THIS BOOK MAKE YOU FEEL?

KID RATING:

PARENT RATING:

THINGS TO REMEMBER:

_____

_____

_____

_____

_____

TITLE:

AUTHOR:

ILLUSTRATOR:

DATE FIRST READ:

WHERE DID WE GET THIS BOOK?

HOW MUCH YOU'VE READ THIS BOOK:

A
LITTLE

A
LOT

HOW DID THIS BOOK MAKE YOU FEEL?

KID RATING:

PARENT RATING:

THINGS TO REMEMBER:

_____

_____

_____

_____

_____

TITLE:

AUTHOR:

ILLUSTRATOR:

DATE FIRST READ:

WHERE DID WE GET THIS BOOK?

HOW MUCH YOU'VE READ THIS BOOK:

A
LITTLE

A
LOT

HOW DID THIS BOOK MAKE YOU FEEL?

KID RATING:

PARENT RATING:

THINGS TO REMEMBER:

_____

_____

_____

_____

_____

TITLE:

AUTHOR:

ILLUSTRATOR:

DATE FIRST READ:

WHERE DID WE GET THIS BOOK?

HOW MUCH YOU'VE READ THIS BOOK:

A
LITTLE

A
LOT

HOW DID THIS BOOK MAKE YOU FEEL?

KID RATING:

PARENT RATING:

THINGS TO REMEMBER:

TITLE:

AUTHOR:

ILLUSTRATOR:

DATE FIRST READ:

WHERE DID WE GET THIS BOOK?

HOW MUCH YOU'VE READ THIS BOOK:

A
LITTLE

A
LOT

HOW DID THIS BOOK MAKE YOU FEEL?

KID RATING:

PARENT RATING:

THINGS TO REMEMBER:

_____

_____

_____

_____

_____

TITLE:

AUTHOR:

ILLUSTRATOR:

DATE FIRST READ:

WHERE DID WE GET THIS BOOK?

HOW MUCH YOU'VE READ THIS BOOK:

A
LITTLE

A
LOT

HOW DID THIS BOOK MAKE YOU FEEL?

KID RATING:

PARENT RATING:

THINGS TO REMEMBER:

_____

_____

_____

_____

_____

TITLE:

AUTHOR:

ILLUSTRATOR:

DATE FIRST READ:

WHERE DID WE GET THIS BOOK?

HOW MUCH YOU'VE READ THIS BOOK:

A
LITTLE

A
LOT

HOW DID THIS BOOK MAKE YOU FEEL?

KID RATING:

PARENT RATING:

THINGS TO REMEMBER:

_____

_____

_____

_____

_____

TITLE:

AUTHOR:

ILLUSTRATOR:

DATE FIRST READ:

WHERE DID WE GET THIS BOOK?

HOW MUCH YOU'VE READ THIS BOOK:

A
LITTLE

A
LOT

HOW DID THIS BOOK MAKE YOU FEEL?

KID RATING:

PARENT RATING:

THINGS TO REMEMBER:

_____

_____

_____

_____

_____

TITLE:

AUTHOR:

ILLUSTRATOR:

DATE FIRST READ:

WHERE DID WE GET THIS BOOK?

HOW MUCH YOU'VE READ THIS BOOK:

A
LITTLE

A
LOT

HOW DID THIS BOOK MAKE YOU FEEL?

KID RATING:

♡ ♡ ♡ ♡ ♡

PARENT RATING:

♡ ♡ ♡ ♡ ♡

THINGS TO REMEMBER:

_____

_____

_____

_____

_____

"Books are a uniquely portable magic."

STEPHEN KING

TITLE:

AUTHOR:

ILLUSTRATOR:

DATE FIRST READ:

WHERE DID WE GET THIS BOOK?

HOW MUCH YOU'VE READ THIS BOOK:

A
LITTLE

A
LOT

HOW DID THIS BOOK MAKE YOU FEEL?

KID RATING:

PARENT RATING:

THINGS TO REMEMBER:

TITLE:

AUTHOR:

ILLUSTRATOR:

DATE FIRST READ:

WHERE DID WE GET THIS BOOK?

HOW MUCH YOU'VE READ THIS BOOK:

A
LITTLE

A
LOT

HOW DID THIS BOOK MAKE YOU FEEL?

KID RATING:

PARENT RATING:

THINGS TO REMEMBER:

_____

_____

_____

_____

_____

TITLE:

AUTHOR:

ILLUSTRATOR:

DATE FIRST READ:

WHERE DID WE GET THIS BOOK?

HOW MUCH YOU'VE READ THIS BOOK:

A
LITTLE

A
LOT

HOW DID THIS BOOK MAKE YOU FEEL?

KID RATING:

♡ ♡ ♡ ♡ ♡

PARENT RATING:

♡ ♡ ♡ ♡ ♡

THINGS TO REMEMBER:

_____

_____

_____

_____

_____

TITLE:

AUTHOR:

ILLUSTRATOR:

DATE FIRST READ:

WHERE DID WE GET THIS BOOK?

HOW MUCH YOU'VE READ THIS BOOK:

A
LITTLE

A
LOT

HOW DID THIS BOOK MAKE YOU FEEL?

KID RATING:

♡ ♡ ♡ ♡ ♡

PARENT RATING:

♡ ♡ ♡ ♡ ♡

THINGS TO REMEMBER:

_____

_____

_____

_____

_____

TITLE:

AUTHOR:

ILLUSTRATOR:

DATE FIRST READ:

WHERE DID WE GET THIS BOOK?

HOW MUCH YOU'VE READ THIS BOOK:

A
LITTLE

A
LOT

HOW DID THIS BOOK MAKE YOU FEEL?

KID RATING:

PARENT RATING:

THINGS TO REMEMBER:

_____

_____

_____

_____

_____

TITLE:

AUTHOR:

ILLUSTRATOR:

DATE FIRST READ:

WHERE DID WE GET THIS BOOK?

HOW MUCH YOU'VE READ THIS BOOK:

A LITTLE

A LOT

HOW DID THIS BOOK MAKE YOU FEEL?

KID RATING:

PARENT RATING:

THINGS TO REMEMBER:

TITLE:

AUTHOR:

ILLUSTRATOR:

DATE FIRST READ:

WHERE DID WE GET THIS BOOK?

HOW MUCH YOU'VE READ THIS BOOK:

A
LITTLE

A
LOT

HOW DID THIS BOOK MAKE YOU FEEL?

KID RATING:

PARENT RATING:

THINGS TO REMEMBER:

_____

_____

_____

_____

_____

TITLE:

AUTHOR:

ILLUSTRATOR:

DATE FIRST READ:

WHERE DID WE GET THIS BOOK?

HOW MUCH YOU'VE READ THIS BOOK:

A
LITTLE

A
LOT

HOW DID THIS BOOK MAKE YOU FEEL?

KID RATING:

PARENT RATING:

THINGS TO REMEMBER:

_____

_____

_____

_____

_____

TITLE:

AUTHOR:

ILLUSTRATOR:

DATE FIRST READ:

WHERE DID WE GET THIS BOOK?

HOW MUCH YOU'VE READ THIS BOOK:

A
LITTLE

A
LOT

HOW DID THIS BOOK MAKE YOU FEEL?

KID RATING:

PARENT RATING:

THINGS TO REMEMBER:

_____

_____

_____

_____

_____

"A BOOK IS LIKE A GARDEN, CARRIED IN THE POCKET."

CHINESE PROVERB

TITLE:

AUTHOR:

ILLUSTRATOR:

DATE FIRST READ:

WHERE DID WE GET THIS BOOK?

HOW MUCH YOU'VE READ THIS BOOK:

A
LITTLE

A
LOT

HOW DID THIS BOOK MAKE YOU FEEL?

KID RATING:

PARENT RATING:

THINGS TO REMEMBER:

_____

_____

_____

_____

_____

TITLE:

AUTHOR:

ILLUSTRATOR:

DATE FIRST READ:

WHERE DID WE GET THIS BOOK?

HOW MUCH YOU'VE READ THIS BOOK:

A
LITTLE

A
LOT

HOW DID THIS BOOK MAKE YOU FEEL?

KID RATING:

PARENT RATING:

THINGS TO REMEMBER:

_____

_____

_____

_____

_____

TITLE:

AUTHOR:

ILLUSTRATOR:

DATE FIRST READ:

WHERE DID WE GET THIS BOOK?

HOW MUCH YOU'VE READ THIS BOOK:

A LITTLE   A LOT

HOW DID THIS BOOK MAKE YOU FEEL?

KID RATING:

♡ ♡ ♡ ♡ ♡

PARENT RATING:

♡ ♡ ♡ ♡ ♡

THINGS TO REMEMBER:

_____

_____

_____

_____

_____

TITLE:

AUTHOR:

ILLUSTRATOR:

DATE FIRST READ:

WHERE DID WE GET THIS BOOK?

HOW MUCH YOU'VE READ THIS BOOK:

A
LITTLE

A
LOT

HOW DID THIS BOOK MAKE YOU FEEL?

KID RATING:

PARENT RATING:

THINGS TO REMEMBER:

_____

_____

_____

_____

_____

TITLE:

AUTHOR:

ILLUSTRATOR:

DATE FIRST READ:

WHERE DID WE GET THIS BOOK?

HOW MUCH YOU'VE READ THIS BOOK:

A
LITTLE

A
LOT

HOW DID THIS BOOK MAKE YOU FEEL?

KID RATING:

PARENT RATING:

THINGS TO REMEMBER:

_____

_____

_____

_____

_____

TITLE:

AUTHOR:

ILLUSTRATOR:

DATE FIRST READ:

WHERE DID WE GET THIS BOOK?

HOW MUCH YOU'VE READ THIS BOOK:

A
LITTLE

A
LOT

HOW DID THIS BOOK MAKE YOU FEEL?

KID RATING:

♡ ♡ ♡ ♡ ♡

PARENT RATING:

♡ ♡ ♡ ♡ ♡

THINGS TO REMEMBER:

_____

_____

_____

_____

_____

TITLE:

AUTHOR:

ILLUSTRATOR:

DATE FIRST READ:

WHERE DID WE GET THIS BOOK?

HOW MUCH YOU'VE READ THIS BOOK:

A
LITTLE

A
LOT

HOW DID THIS BOOK MAKE YOU FEEL?

KID RATING:

PARENT RATING:

THINGS TO REMEMBER:

TITLE:

AUTHOR:

ILLUSTRATOR:

DATE FIRST READ:

WHERE DID WE GET THIS BOOK?

HOW MUCH YOU'VE READ THIS BOOK:

A
LITTLE

A
LOT

HOW DID THIS BOOK MAKE YOU FEEL?

KID RATING:

PARENT RATING:

THINGS TO REMEMBER:

_____

_____

_____

_____

_____

TITLE:

AUTHOR:

ILLUSTRATOR:

DATE FIRST READ:

WHERE DID WE GET THIS BOOK?

HOW MUCH YOU'VE READ THIS BOOK:

A
LITTLE

A
LOT

HOW DID THIS BOOK MAKE YOU FEEL?

KID RATING:

PARENT RATING:

THINGS TO REMEMBER:

TITLE:

AUTHOR:

ILLUSTRATOR:

DATE FIRST READ:

WHERE DID WE GET THIS BOOK?

HOW MUCH YOU'VE READ THIS BOOK:

A
LITTLE

A
LOT

HOW DID THIS BOOK MAKE YOU FEEL?

KID RATING:

PARENT RATING:

THINGS TO REMEMBER:

_____

_____

_____

_____

_____

TITLE:

AUTHOR:

ILLUSTRATOR:

DATE FIRST READ:

WHERE DID WE GET THIS BOOK?

HOW MUCH YOU'VE READ THIS BOOK:

A
LITTLE

A
LOT

HOW DID THIS BOOK MAKE YOU FEEL?

KID RATING:

♡ ♡ ♡ ♡ ♡

PARENT RATING:

♡ ♡ ♡ ♡ ♡

THINGS TO REMEMBER:

_____

_____

_____

_____

_____

TITLE:

AUTHOR:

ILLUSTRATOR:

DATE FIRST READ:

WHERE DID WE GET THIS BOOK?

HOW MUCH YOU'VE READ THIS BOOK:

A
LITTLE

A
LOT

HOW DID THIS BOOK MAKE YOU FEEL?

KID RATING:

PARENT RATING:

THINGS TO REMEMBER:

_____

_____

_____

_____

_____

Reading Lists

Books Are Magic List

BY ABBY RAUSCHER
(children's book buyer)

Books Are Magic is Emma Straub's beloved independent bookstore in Cobble Hill, Brooklyn. In this list, children's book buyer Abby Rauscher takes on the difficult task of choosing eight house favorites, representing books recommended across all age groups.

☐ *The Watermelon Seed*
by Greg Pizzoli / ages 3–5

The Watermelon Seed is my absolute favorite go-to for story time; it is always a hit. The clean illustrations are vibrant enough to hold any squirmy baby's attention, and it's always so fun to act out the poor gator's despair when it—gasp—swallows a seed!

☐ *Nanette's Baguette*
by Mo Willems / ages 3–5

It takes a bit of practice to read this tongue twister aloud just right, but that's half the fun! Stumble through Nanette's journey to pick up a fresh baguette from Juliette the baker, and see what happens after she devours the entire wonderful loaf before returning home to her mother.

☐ *Bark, George*
by Jules Feiffer / ages 4–8

The humor in this book is pitch-perfect for preschoolers and kindergartners. A puppy named George can do just about anything but bark: He meows, quacks, oinks, and moos. The animal sounds make it accessible for toddlers, who will joyfully bark along.

☐ *The Day You Begin*
by Jacqueline Woodson,
ill. by Rafael López / ages 5–8

This picture book is about finding beauty in the things that make you *you* and joy in things that are so wonderfully different from you. López's illustrations are dreamlike and so exquisitely detailed that there's always something new to discover on each spread.

☐ *Dragons in a Bag*
by Zetta Elliot,
ill. by Geneva B / ages 8–12

While Jaxon's mom is out looking for work, he spends the day with an old lady who has baby dragons in her handbag. Jax and his friends are charged with delivering the dragons to a magical land, but the little beasts escape, and a crazy romp ensues.

☐ *Some Places More than Others*
by Renée Watson / ages 8–12

This quiet novel is a gorgeous examination of family, history, and the roots that both ground us and allow us to grow. Watson's beautiful and exacting prose conveys her gentle understanding of the complex histories that entwine and conspire to make us who we are.

☐ *Lumberjanes*
by Noelle Stevenson, Shannon Watters, Grace Ellis, and Brooklyn Allen / ages 9–12

If your kid loves adventure, magic, and cool things in general, they're going to adore *Lumberjanes*! This graphic-novel series follows the escapades of five best friends at sleepaway camp. It's a fantastic display of the many strange and wonderful ways that girls can move through the world. After reading the comics, pick up the amazing spin-off novel series by Mariko Tamaki, also illustrated by Brooklyn Allen!

☐ *Pet*
by Akwaeke Emezi / ages 12 & up

Pet is nothing short of breathtaking. It's a critical examination of the society we live in today, of the future we hope to create, and of the enduring need to keep our eyes and hearts open to the most vulnerable among us. This novel deals with some heavy, complicated issues: I'd generally recommend it for the strictly 12-and-up crowd.

BOOKS ABOUT
epic adventures

From magical quests to exploring the ordinary, these stories are action-packed and full of unexpected twists and turns. Sure to excite even the pickiest reader, this list will make your child want to keep reading!

Add your own favorites:

_____

_____

_____

☐ *Small in the City*
by Sydney Smith / ages 4–8

An emotive and unfurling tale of a boy exploring a big city. With masterful storytelling and idyllic illustrations, this is a compelling story about seeing the gigantic world through little eyes.

**SARAH YEWMAN,
picture books blogger**

☐ *Today*
by Julie Morstad / ages 4–8

An interactive picture book where each day is a new day with a new decision the reader can make. Read it over and over to spark conversation over the possibilities a day can bring.

**KELLIE DIGUANGCO,
Secret Society of Books**

☐ *Truman*
**by Jean Reidy,
ill. by Lucy Ruth Cummins / ages 4–8**

When Truman's girl, Sarah, leaves for her first day of school, his impatience for her to come back causes him to attempt the impossible: crossing the apartment to look for her. A tale of determination and friendship.

**MELISSA POSTEN,
the Novel Neighbor**

☐ *Zog and the Flying Doctors*
by Julia Donaldson,
ill. by Axel Scheffler / ages 4–8

Princess Pearl is a doctor, but her
uncle, the king, wants her to act like
a traditional princess. A fun and
fantastical story with lessons about
feminism and friendship!

SARA WIGGLESWORTH,
Green Apple Books

☐ *Sweep*
by Jonathan Auxier / ages 8–12

Chimney sweep Nan Sparrow doesn't
realize she needs saving until a bit
of magic brings Charlie into her life.
Auxier's spellbinding writing wraps
itself around you like a blanket and
redefines what family can be.

MELISSA POSTEN,
the Novel Neighbor

☐ *Pax*
by Sara Pennypacker,
ill. by Jon Klassen / ages 8–12

When Peter and his fox, Pax, are
separated by an impending war,
they fight to be reunited. Both face
an epic journey that will test and
ultimately reunite them.

SAM MILLER,
Carmichael's Bookstore

☐ *The Adventurer's Guide to Successful Escapes*
by Wade Albert White / ages 9–12

Anne and Penelope are orphans who
desperately want to be adventurers,
so they bust out of their terrible
orphanage and into a new school—
only to find that it's nothing like they
thought it would be.

ABBY RAUSCHER,
Books Are Magic

☐ The *Voyage to Magical North*
by Claire Fayers / ages 8–12

Two kids find themselves on a
legendary pirate ship heading to
a magical island in this enchanting
fantasy novel. Fun, funny, and thrilling!

NICOLE BRINKLEY,
Oblong Books & Music

☐ *Look Both Ways*
by Jason Reynolds / ages 10–14

This collection of ten interwoven
short stories takes place at a middle
school's dismissal time. Readers will
look closely at the world around
them and realize each person they
see has a story to tell.

CATHY BERNER,
Blue Willow Bookshop

BOOKS ABOUT
cultures around the world

Reading enables us to explore a wider world and better understand what it is like to walk in another person's shoes. These empathy-building stories show how the world looks from many points of view.

☐ *Say Hello!*
by Rachel Isadora /ages 3–5

A cute story about a little girl walking through her neighborhood. She says hello to all of her neighbors in a variety of languages. A beautiful way to portray diversity and inclusion!

SARA WIGGLESWORTH,
Green Apple Books

☐ *Lunch at 10 Pomegranate Street*
by Felicita Sala / ages 3–10

A diverse and accessible recipe book, celebrating food and culture across the globe. This book encourages and inspires readers to make new dishes and embrace different tastes and styles in their own home.

SARAH YEWMAN,
picture books blogger

☐ *Sweetest Kulu*
by Celina Kalluk,
ill. by Alexandria Neonakis / ages 0–3

A lyrical Inuit bedtime story about the gifts animals give to a newborn baby. There are striking illustrations of each creature as they visit to offer values like tenderness, creativity, and love.

CHRISTINE UTZ,
Magers & Quinn Booksellers

☐ *La Princesa and the Pea*
by Susan Middleton Elya,
ill. by Juana Martinez-Neal /
ages 4–8

A rhyming, Latino twist on the classic fairy tale "The Princess and the Pea." In this delightful bilingual retelling, Spanish and English words are intertwined throughout the text.

MAYA LE ESPIRITU,
MaiStoryBook

☐ The Proudest Blue
by Ibtihaj Muhammed and S. K. Ali, ill. by Hatem Aly / ages 4–10

Faizah's older sister, Asiya, wears a hijab to school for the first time. This story is told from Faizah's perspective as she observes the strength Asiya portrays, even in the face of unkindness.

CATHY BERNER,
Blue Willow Bookshop

☐ Other Words for Home
by Jasmine Warga / ages 8–12

Jude and her mother move from Syria to Cincinnati, where Jude must navigate a new school, a new identity, and the auditions for the school play. A charming and powerful novel-in-verse about claiming your place.

NICOLE BRINKLEY,
Oblong Books & Music

☐ Juana and Lucas
by Juana Medina / ages 5–8

Juana likes drawing, Brussels sprouts, and her dog, Lucas, but she does not like learning English. In this engaging bilingual chapter book, you will experience a day in the life of a girl living in Bogotá, Colombia.

CHRISTINE UTZ,
Magers & Quinn Booksellers

— ABRAMS' Favorite —

☐ Danza!
by Duncan Tonatiuh / ages 6–10

A picture book celebrating the famous dancer and choreographer Amalia Hernández and the rich history of dance in Mexico.

☐ The Journey
by Francesca Sanna / ages 5–8

Explore one family's escape from danger in their homeland and the journey they endure together as they search for safety. A read-aloud story that can help start discussions about humanity, safety, and refugee experiences.

MAYA LE ESPIRITU,
MaiStoryBook

Add your own favorites:

_____

_____

_____

BOOKS ABOUT
earth

Celebrate our planet every day with books that introduce children to the environment and help them understand nature. They will be inspired to help take care of the Earth any way they can!

Add your own favorites:

_____

_____

_____

□ *They All Saw a Cat*
by Brendan Wenzel / ages 3–6

A cat walks through its world where each animal sees the cat differently. By exploring each character's perspective of the cat through vivid illustrations, Wenzel celebrates how all living things are connected.

CATHY BERNER,
Blue Willow Bookshop

□ *Here We Are: Notes for Living on Planet Earth*
by Oliver Jeffers / ages 3–7

A perfect story to welcome your little ones to the world. This gorgeous guide to life on Earth introduces elements of our planet, while celebrating the vast diversity of those who call this planet home.

MAYA LE ESPIRITU,
MaiStoryBook

□ *Dandy*
by Ame Dyckman,
ill. by Charles Santoso / ages 4–8

The story of a father trying to destroy a dandelion growing in his perfect lawn while his daughter tries to save and befriend it. This book has a valuable message and breathtaking illustrations.

AMANDA MALDONADO,
Carmichael's Bookstore

☐ The Honeybee

by Kirsten Hall,
ill. by Isabelle Arsenault / ages 4–8

This buzzing, vibrant picture book
introduces kids to one of the most
important creatures in the world.
A perfect read-aloud introduction
to the life of a bee!

NICOLE BRINKLEY,
Oblong Books & Music

☐ The Brilliant Deep

by Kate Messner,
ill. by Matthew Forsythe / ages 5–8

The true story behind Ken Nedimyer
learning how to save coral reefs with
a hammer, glue, and newly grown
coral. Educational, inspirational, and
beautifully illustrated.

NICOLE BRINKLEY,
Oblong Books & Music

☐ Earth! My First 4.54 Billion Years

by Stacy McAnulty,
ill. by David Litchfield / ages 4–8

A joyful story told from the perspective
of planet Earth. Each page is filled
with facts from Earth, including her
family history, her love of humans,
and gentle reminders to take better
care of the planet.

DAMITA NOCTON,
the Country Bookshop

☐ Saving Wonder

by Mary Knight / ages 8–12

Curley Hines's grandfather teaches
him a word a week in hopes Curley
can someday leave their tiny coal-
mining town. Instead, the mining
company threatens their family
mountain, and Curley must use the
words to fight.

SAM MILLER,
Carmichael's Bookstore

☐ Camilla, Cartographer

by Julie Dillemuth,
ill. by Laura Wood / ages 4–8

Camilla loves maps of all kinds, so
when the snow falls too deep to find
the paths, she delights in making a
new map to help her friend Parsley
find the path to the creek. Warm
illustrations bring this book to life.

ANGIE MURCHISON TALLY,
the Country Bookshop

— ABRAMS' Favorite —

☐ Deep in the Ocean

by Lucie Brunellière / ages 3–5

This beautiful board book takes
readers on a journey through
fascinating water by exploring
colorful sea creatures and
mysterious waters.

BOOKS ABOUT
bodies

These kid-friendly books about the human body turn complicated topics into leaing opportunities with age-appropriate words and exciting illustrations.

☐ *Lucha Libre: Anatomy/Anatomía*
by Patty Rodriguez and Ariana Stein, ill. by Citlali Reyes / ages 2–5

What better way to learn the parts of the body than through the colorful world of lucha libre? This bilingual board book is perfect for teaching children the words for knee, elbow, and more.

**NICOLE BRINKLEY,
Oblong Books & Music**

☐ *Skulls!*
by Blair Thornburgh, ill. by Scott Campbell / ages 4–8

This book presents a positive look into a very important part of our bodies: the skull. The information in the main text focuses on the science of the skull in a fun and lighthearted way.

**AMANDA MALDONADO,
Carmichael's Bookstore**

☐ *Toesy Toes*
by Sarah Tsiang / ages 0–2

With silly rhyming couplets and photos of diverse babies, this adorable board book celebrates the different sensations a baby might experience with their toes.

**CHRISTINE UTZ,
Magers & Quinn Booksellers**

☐ *Hair Love*
by Matthew A. Cherry, ill. by Vashti Harrison / ages 4–8

In this charming picture book, Zuri describes how her hair has a mind of its own. When she needs help with it, Zuri and her father collaborate to create the hairstyle she wants for the day.

**CATHY BERNER,
Blue Willow Bookshop**

☐ *Frida Kahlo and Her Animalitos*
by Monica Brown,
ill. by John Parra / ages 4–8

Kahlo and her animalitos represent the rich heritage of Mexican culture and the strength of women, and normalize living and working with illness and disability.

SARA WIGGLESWORTH,
Green Apple Books

☐ *It's Perfectly Normal*
by Robie H. Harris,
ill. by Michael Emberley / ages 10 & up

This matter-of-fact guide to changing bodies and sex offers current and correct information written clearly and without judgment for tweens and teens. It can help answer questions and make difficult conversations easier.

SAM MILLER,
Carmichael's Bookstore

☐ *Sex Is a Funny Word*
by Cory Silverberg,
ill. by Fiona Smyth / ages 7–10

A fun, engaging, and important book for kids and their caregivers about bodies, gender, and sexuality; it is inclusive and informative without preaching.

BREIN LOPEZ,
Children's Book World

Add your own favorites:

_____

_____

_____

_____

_____

_____

_____

☐ *Anatomicum*
by Jennifer Z. Paxton,
ill. by Katy Wiedemann / ages 9–11

Take a closer look at your body by learning everything from which muscles express emotion to how food is processed in your digestive system. Understand the basics with help from a succinct narrative and delicate illustrations.

SARAH YEWMAN,
picture books blogger

BOOKS ABOUT
tough emotions

Some feelings are more difficult to handle than others, and often these emotions can make children uncomfortable. These books will open up conversations about anger, sadness, loneliness, grief, and fear.

☐ *When Sadness Is at Your Door*
by Eva Eland / ages 3–7

This is a simple book to introduce the idea of sadness to young children. Sadness is a visitor you can engage with by sitting quietly, drawing, or going on a walk.

**AMANDA MALDONADO,
Carmichael's Bookstore**

☐ *Grandpa's Stories*
by Joseph Coelho,
ill. by Allison Colpoys / ages 4–8

This tender book captures the special relationship between a grandparent and grandchild. Although this is a story about death, the colorful pictures and hopeful ending provide reassurance.

**ROSEMARY D'URSO,
LibraryMom.com**

☐ *The Rabbit Listened*
by Cori Doerrfeld / ages 3–5

Something sad happens and all of the animals try to tell Taylor how to feel. Then the rabbit comes along and just listens. A deeply moving exploration of grief and empathy.

**CHRISTINE UTZ,
Magers & Quinn Booksellers**

☐ *Ida, Always*
by Caron Levis,
ill. by Charles Santoso / ages 4–8

Ida and Gus are best friends who spend every day together. Then, Gus learns that Ida is sick and will not be getting better. A beautiful reminder that the ones we love are always with us.

**RAE ANN PARKER,
Parnassus Books**

☐ *Mum's Jumper*
by Jayde Perkin / ages 4 & up

A sensitive, but honestly written account about loss, grief, and empathy. Perkin carefully broaches the topic of death with a younger audience using rare honesty, warmth, and understanding.

SARAH YEWMAN,
picture books blogger

☐ *The Thing About Jellyfish*
by Ali Benjamin / ages 12 & up

A wise and knowing story about grappling with bereavement, making peace with loss, and learning how to cope with the ebb and flow of friendship. A good, sad read.

SAM MILLER,
Carmichael's Bookstore

☐ *Pilu of the Woods*
by Mai K. Nguyen / ages 8–12

Willow finds a lost tree spirit named Pilu and decides to help her get back home—but Pilu isn't ready to go back. A beautiful, poignant look at grief and coping with anxiety and loneliness.

NICOLE BRINKLEY,
Oblong Books & Music

Add your own favorites:

_____

_____

_____

_____

_____

_____

_____

_____

☐ *The Line Tender*
by Kate Allen / ages 10 & up

One summer, great white sharks start appearing off the coast of Lucy's town and everything changes. This novel has humor, grief, friendship, marine biology, and a whole lot of heart.

CHRISTINE UTZ,
Magers & Quinn Booksellers

BOOKS ABOUT
mindfulness

Help your kids express their emotions in healthy ways. By celebrating love and teaching resilience, these books will help readers find kindness, happiness, and patience in every situation.

☐ *When Grandma Gives You a Lemon Tree*
by Jamie L. B. Deenihan,
ill. by Lorraine Rocha / ages 3–7

This book cleverly takes the proverbial phrase "When life gives you lemons, make lemonade!" and incorporates it into a child-friendly story teaching resilience and self-reliance. An entertaining story with humorous text, colorful illustrations, and important life lessons.

ROSEMARY D'URSO,
LibraryMom.com

☐ *Can I Be Your Dog?*
by Troy Cummings / ages 3–7

Arfy is a lonely, homeless dog with a plan. Featuring the lost art of letter writing, this book follows Arfy as he searches for a home. It will warm any child's heart.

LAUREN SAVAGE,
the Reading Bug

☐ *In My Heart*
by Jo Witek,
ill. by Christine Roussey / ages 2–4
We can feel so many different feelings. Toddlers and young children will enjoy the simple illustrations in this book accompanied by words that can help them communicate their emotions.

AMANDA MALDONADO,
Carmichael's Bookstore

☐ *I Am Love*
by Susan Verde,
ill. by Peter H. Reynolds / ages 3–7

A celebration of love that teaches readers to look inward to find kindness, compassion, gratitude, and self-love. *I Am Love* gives readers actionable steps to spread love wherever they go.

VERA AHIYYA,
the Tutu Teacher

□ *The Fate of Fausto*
by Oliver Jeffers / ages 4–8

The story of a man who claims everything he sees as "his."
A cautionary fable about greed, arrogance, and the fate that ensues. This book speaks truth to not recognizing when you have enough.

KELLIE DIGUANGCO,
Secret Society of Books

□ *Tar Beach*
by Faith Ringgold / ages 4–8

Nighttime in the city is a magical hour, especially on tar beach, a perch high above the noise of the streets. It is where Cassie Louise Lightfoot loves to share stories and laughter with her family.

ANGIE MURCHISON TALLY,
the Country Bookshop

□ *After the Fall*
by Dan Santat / ages 4–8

Humpty Dumpty is back again! Although his cracks from the fall are healed, something is still broken on the inside. This book encourages children to face their challenges one step at a time.

MAYA LE ESPIRITU,
MaiStoryBook

Add your own favorites:

_____

_____

_____

_____

_____

_____

_____

□ *Life on Mars*
by Jon Agee / ages 4–8

An original and cleverly observed narrative, supported by shrewd visual humor. This trip to Mars might not be all it's cracked up to be, but with a little patience it could be epic!

SARAH YEWMAN,
picture books blogger

BOOKS THAT ARE
funny

Want to give your kids the giggles? Perfect for a rainy day, family time, or a silly story time, these hilarious stories will make everyone laugh out loud.

Add your own favorites:

_____

_____

_____

☐ *Barnyard Dance!*
by Sandra Boynton / ages 0–3

Stomp your feet and clap your hands for this rollicking, rhythmic romp around the barnyard that is an absolute must for every child's first bookshelf.

ANGIE MURCHISON TALLY,
the Country Bookshop

☐ *Mother Bruce*
by Ryan T. Higgins / ages 3–5

Bruce is a bear who likes to eat eggs. One day, he finds a recipe for hard-boiled goose eggs, but he doesn't cook the eggs long enough and they hatch! A hilarious picture book.

CATHY BERNER,
Blue Willow Bookshop

☐ *Where Is the Green Sheep?*
by Mem Fox,
ill. by Judy Horacek / ages 4–7

Searching for the green sheep is a joy for kids and their parents in this delightful book! There are lots of giggle-worthy moments and adorable illustrations.

AMANDA MALDONADO,
Carmichael's Bookstore

☐ **There's a Dinosaur on the 13th Floor**
by Wade Bradford,
ill. by Kevin Hawkes / ages 4–8

Will Mr. Snore rest on *any* floor of the Sharemore Hotel? All he wants is some peace and quiet! An all-around fun and silly book with a simple funny twist at the end.

LAUREN SAVAGE,
the Reading Bug

☐ **Haggis and Tank Unleashed series**
by Jessica Young,
ill. by James Burks / ages 5–7

Two dog friends, tiny Haggis and large Tank, go on wild adventures in their backyard. Their big imaginations take them sailing with pirates, hunting for dinosaurs, and so much more!

RAE ANN PARKER,
Parnassus Books

☐ **There Are No Bears in This Bakery**
by Julia Sarcone-Roach / ages 4–8

Tough cat Muffin investigates a mysterious growling in the neighborhood bakery. Told through Muffin's classic hard-boiled narration, this noir picture book is chuckle-worthy and ripe for rereading!

SAM MILLER,
Carmichael's Bookstore

☐ **The Treehouse series**
by Andy Griffiths,
ill. by Terry Denton / ages 8–12

Andy and Terry live in the most amazing treehouse! It has a shark tank and trampoline room, and keeps getting cooler. This hybrid graphic-novel series will have kids laughing all the way past the 117th story.

ANGIE MURCHISON TALLY,
the Country Bookshop

☐ **The Wolf, the Duck, and the Mouse**
by Mac Barnett,
ill. by Jon Klassen / ages 4–8

A clever tale about a mouse who is eaten by a wolf, only to find a duck already living in the wolf's belly. This picture book reminds readers to find a creative solution to any circumstance.

CATHY BERNER,
Blue Willow Bookshop

☐ **Frazzled**
by Booki Vivat / ages 8–12

Middle child Abbie Wu is always frazzled, which makes her new life as a middle schooler hard to handle. Vivat conveys melodrama and hilarity through black-and-white illustrations and doodles.

MELISSA POSTEN,
the Novel Neighbor

BOOKS ABOUT
learning & creativity

This selection of books is sure to spark ideas and inspire creativity in children. These stories not only encourage imagination and curiosity, they also empower kids to embrace what is unique about themselves.

☐ *Art*
by Patrick McDonnell / ages 3–6

This lovely picture book is a celebration of art and imagination. It inspires children to zig, zag, scribble, and squiggle with quirky wordplay and vibrant images.

AMANDA MALDONADO,
Carmichael's Bookstore

☐ *The Book of Mistakes*
by Corinna Luyken / ages 4–8

The biggest killer of creativity is the fear of failure. This picture book for all ages turns mistakes into happy accidents and allows for persistence and play to transform what may seem like a small error into a massive, breathtaking masterpiece.

ABBY RAUSCHER,
Books Are Magic

☐ *All the Ways to Be Smart*
by Davina Bell,
ill. by Allison Colpoys / ages 3–6

There are so many ways to be smart! This book is a celebration of the unique talents and qualities that make children who they are. Empowerment and encouragement at its finest.

KELLIE DIGUANGCO,
Secret Society of Books

☐ *What If . . .*
by Samantha Berger,
ill. by Mike Curato / ages 4–8

Mixed-media artwork combined with rhythmic prose is perfect for inspiring a passion for creativity in any little one. Children will be encouraged to expand their art beyond pencil and paper in this book.

MAYA LE ESPIRITU,
MaiStoryBook

☐ *Yasmin in Charge*
by Saadia Faruqi,
ill. by Hatem Aly / ages 5–8

Yasmin, a resourceful young Pakistani girl, is always looking to solve life's problems. She finds creative solutions to everyday challenges using inspiration from her surroundings and her imagination.

CHRISTINE UTZ,
Magers & Quinn Booksellers

☐ *Calling All Minds*
by Temple Grandin / ages 8 & up

World-renowned inventor and autism spokesperson Temple Grandin shares the learning habits of many of the world's leading thinkers, tells her own story, and provides experiments to encourage kids to tinker on their own.

BREIN LOPEZ,
Children's Book World

☐ *Dr. Seuss's Horse Museum*
by Dr. Seuss,
ill. by Andrew Joyner / ages 7 & up

The museum in the book offers thirty-three different artistic interpretations of a horse, from cave paintings to early photography. This overview will help readers understand what art is and how to find it in everyday life.

SAM MILLER,
Carmichael's Bookstore

ABRAMS' Favorite

☐ *The Questioneers series*
by Andrea Beaty,
ill. by David Roberts / ages 5–7

Meet Rosie, Iggy, Ada, and Sofia, and follow their adventures as they explore engineering, architecture, science, and activism. A moving series of picture books and chapter books that inspires readers of all ages to lead, question, and think!

☐ *The Dictionary of Difficult Words*
by Jane Solomon,
ill. by Louise Lockhart / ages 7–12

This book introduces four hundred intriguing words with facts and examples to contextualize them. Readers will become grandiloquent speakers and fall in love with learning new words.

KELLIE DIGUANGCO,
Secret Society of Books

Add your own favorites:

_____

_____

_____

BOOKS ABOUT
school

Help your child prepare and be excited for school by reading thoughtful stories that will help them dream big and learn key lessons of friendship, sharing, and perseverance.

☐ *We Don't Eat Our Classmates*
by Ryan T. Higgins / ages 3–5

How does Penelope the T. rex start her first day of school? She greets her new classmates by eating them, of course! Penelope proves that even after a rough start, you can make friends through sharing, kindness, and playing!

**MAYA LE ESPIRITU,
MaiStoryBook**

☐ *Take Your Pet to School Day*
by Linda Ashman,
ill. by Suzanne Kaufman / ages 3–5

Cats, dogs, guinea pigs, horses, even snakes are welcome at Maple View Elementary on Take Your Pet to School Day, but things don't go quite as planned. This book is perfect back-to-school fun with a twist!

**ANGIE MURCHISON TALLY,
the Country Bookshop**

☐ *The King of Kindergarten*
by Derrick Barnes, ill. by
Vanessa Brantley-Newton / ages 3–5

The King of Kindergarten is ready to travel by big yellow carriage to the new kingdom of school. He eats a good breakfast, dresses himself, and is excited to learn. This book makes returning to school fun!

**RAE ANN PARKER,
Parnassus Books**

☐ *Library Lion*
by Michelle Knudsen,
ill. by Kevin Hawkes / ages 4–7

When a lion walks into story time, he certainly stands out! This story challenges why sometimes rules should be broken and stresses the importance of thinking for yourself.

**MELISSA POSTEN,
the Novel Neighbor**

☐ *School's First Day of School*
by Adam Rex,
ill. by Christian Robinson / ages 4–8

A thoughtful story from a school's point of view! This sweet tale of a school opening for the first time conveys the school's anxieties and excitement for housing children.

CATHY BERNER,
Blue Willow Bookshop

☐ *El Deafo*
by Cece Bell / ages 8–10

Going to school and making new friends while wearing a bulky hearing aid can be really tough. Thankfully, Cece has superpowers! This poignant graphic-novel memoir shows how one girl navigates the challenges of her disability.

☐ *If I Built a School*
by Chris Van Dusen / ages 5–8

A boy dreams of designing his own school that includes hover desks and field trips to Mars. The upbeat rhymes and illustrations filled with eye-catching details are sure to result in multiple readings.

ROSEMARY D'URSO,
LibraryMom.com

Add your own favorites:

_____

_____

_____

_____

_____

_____

_____

☐ *The Best at It*
by Maulik Pancholy / ages 8–12

Middle school is hard, and Rahul is looking at a pretty tough year. Supported by his friends and family, Rahul tries to figure out who he is and what he's best at.

CATHY BERNER,
Blue Willow Bookshop

BOOKS ABOUT
feeling or being different

Everyone has a unique story to tell. Whether they don't quite fit in or are striving to be their own unique person, the characters in these books are fearlessly pursuing what makes them happy.

Add your own favorites:

_____

_____

_____

☐ *The Suitcase*
by Chris Naylor-Ballesteros / ages 2–5

When a new animal arrives pulling a big suitcase, the other animals are very curious about what could be inside. This story gently shows tolerance and kindness for others.

**SARAH YEWMAN,
picture books blogger**

☐ *Miss Spider's Tea Party*
by David Kirk / ages 3–6

When lonely Miss Spider invites the neighborhood beetles, flies, and moths to tea, everyone is terrified. But after one small moth takes the chance to trust someone very different from himself, doors open to new friendships.

**ANGIE MURCHISON TALLY,
the Country Bookshop**

☐ *Business Pig*
by Andrea Zuill / ages 3–7

At the animal sanctuary, Jasper knows he's not like the other animals. He would much rather conduct a meeting than splash in the mud, but that doesn't stop him from finding his forever home.

**NICOLE BRINKLEY,
Oblong Books & Music**

☐ *Julián Is a Mermaid*
by Jessica Love / ages 4–8

Julián is inspired when he sees people dressed as mermaids on the train, so he decides to turn himself into a beautiful mermaid by using everyday objects to make his costume. This book encourages self-love and creative expression.

**SARA WIGGLESWORTH,
Green Apple Books**

☐ *The War That Saved My Life*
by Kimberly Brubaker Bradley / ages 8–12

Ten-year-old Ada has never stepped outside of her family's one-bedroom apartment because her mother is embarrassed of her twisted foot. Her life changes after escaping to the country with her brother during the London Blitz.

**RAE ANN PARKER,
Parnassus Books**

☐ *Dreamers*
by Yuyi Morales / ages 4–8

A semi-autobiographical story about Yuyi and her son, Kelly, who emigrate from Mexico to the United States. Everything is unfamiliar and they don't speak English, but a magical place helps them to find solace in their new home.

**SARA WIGGLESWORTH,
Green Apple Books**

☐ *Rain Reign*
by Ann M. Martin / ages 9–12

An astute examination of the blessings and curses of living on the autistic spectrum, the true meaning of home, and what it means to sacrifice for love.

**SAM MILLER,
Carmichael's Bookstore**

☐ *Pokko and the Drum*
by Matthew Forsythe / ages 4–8

Pokko loves her drum, but her parents don't appreciate the noise. She tries hard to be quiet, but she can't help herself! A great example of individuality and tenacity.

**SARAH YEWMAN,
picture books blogger**

☐ *Free Lunch*
by Rex Ogle / ages 11–14

This memoir captures poverty in America. Along with the usual middle-school challenges, Rex's mother signs him up for the school's free-meal program, a situation that he struggles with.

**CATHY BERNER,
Blue Willow Bookshop**

BOOKS ABOUT
responsibility and teamwork

From picking up their toys to holding together their families and communities, these stories show that young people can have an impact on the world around them.

☐ *The Squirrels Who Squabbled*
by Rachel Bright, ill. by Jim Field / ages 3–6

Two greedy squirrels chase the very last pinecone of the season. Can they learn to work together? A funny story about friendship and sharing.

LAUREN SAVAGE, the Reading Bug

☐ *Otto and Pio*
by Marianne Dubuc / ages 3–7

While not explicitly a book about getting a new sibling, it has a similar theme. Otto learns about responsibility for the new Pio as they figure out how to love and take care of each other!

SARA WIGGLESWORTH, Green Apple Books

☐ *Llama Llama Mess Mess Mess*
by Anna Dewdney, ill. by Reed Duncan / ages 2–5

When little Llama refuses to pick up his toys, his mama encourages him to imagine what it would be like if she didn't clean up. The results are hilarious.

ROSEMARY D'URSO, LibraryMom.com

☐ *Mia Mayhem Is a Superhero!*
by Kara West, ill. by Leeza Hernandez / ages 5 & up

Mia Mayhem has just discovered that she's a superhero! This fun chapter book series explores Mia's powers and how she must work with her friends to conquer difficult obstacles.

NICOLE BRINKLEY, Oblong Books & Music

☐ *A Bike Like Sergio's*
by Maribeth Boelts,
ill. by Noah Z. Jones / ages 6–10

A young boy finds money that would enable him to buy his dream bike, but could doing so hurt his integrity? A beautiful moral lesson with opportunities for exploring responsible decisions and one's impact on others.

BREIN LOPEZ,
Children's Book World

☐ *Ghost*
by Jason Reynolds / ages 9–12

Reynolds is a master storyteller who creates characters that are raw and honest. Ghost and his fellow members of the travel track team all come from wildly different backgrounds, but have one thing in common: running.

ANGIE MURCHISON TALLY,
the Country Bookshop

☐ *Just Like Jackie*
by Lindsey Stoddard / ages 8–12

Forced to go to group therapy after getting into a fistfight at school, Robbie struggles to open up about the responsibility she feels for her grandpa.

SAM MILLER,
Carmichael's Bookstore

☐ *Snapdragon*
by Kat Leyh / ages 10 & up

When Snap becomes an apprentice to the so-called witch of the woods, she discovers that magic is real. This graphic novel tackles hard topics while never shying away from the fantastical.

NICOLE BRINKLEY,
Oblong Books & Music

☐ *Nikki on the Line*
by Barbara Carroll Roberts /
ages 9–12

Thirteen-year-old Nikki is thrilled to make an elite travel basketball team, but it comes with stress that is hard to deal with. This story has an authentic voice and a wonderfully diverse group of family and friends.

CATHY BERNER,
Blue Willow Bookshop

Add your own favorites:

_____

_____

_____

BOOKS ABOUT
families

These titles celebrate all kinds of families and their lives together. Whether these characters are frustrated with their families or love them, these stories represent important support systems.

Add your own favorites:

_____

_____

_____

☐ *Once Upon a Goat*
**by Dan Richards,
ill. by Eric Barclay / ages 3–7**

The king and queen ask their fairy godmother for a "kid." Be careful what you wish for! This is the perfect book for all kinds of families.

**LAUREN SAVAGE,
the Reading Bug**

☐ *The Baby Tree*
by Sophie Blackall / ages 3–7

Babies are so mysterious—where do they come from, and why do they appear? Sophie Blackall plays with that question in this sweet story about a kiddo who isn't quite sure where and how her new family member is going to show up.

**EMMA STRAUB,
Books Are Magic**

☐ *A Different Pond*
**by Bao Phi,
ill. by Thi Bui / ages 5–10**

An immigrant father and son (refugees from Vietnam) awake early one morning to go fishing in their new home of Minnesota. The special time shared together reveals old stories from their past and new dreams for their future.

**BREIN LOPEZ,
Children's Book World**

☐ *Mango Moon*
by Diane de Anda,
ill. by Sue Cornelison / ages 7–10

This book shows the emotional trauma of deportation. Maricela and her family try to make sense of their lives without their father, as they grieve and wonder what will come next.

VERA AHIYYA,
the Tutu Teacher

☐ *Front Desk*
by Kelly Yang / ages 8–12

An incredible treatise on community and solidarity. Mia Tang, a young immigrant girl, is determined to win a writing contest in order to help her family escape their coldhearted landlord.

ABBY RAUSCHER,
Books Are Magic

☐ *Song for a Whale*
by Lynne Kelly / ages 8–12

When tech-savvy Iris learns about the lonely whale Blue 55, she decides to create a song for him. This gorgeous, thoughtful novel about a young deaf girl is a must-read adventure.

NICOLE BRINKLEY,
Oblong Books & Music

☐ *As Brave as You*
by Jason Reynolds / ages 10 & up

Two brothers leave Brooklyn to spend the summer with their grandparents while their parents work to fix their marriage. Funny and beautifully written, this is a character-driven story about family and discovering your own kind of bravery.

CHRISTINE UTZ,
Magers & Quinn Booksellers

☐ *Dream Within a Dream*
by Patricia MacLachlan / ages 8–12

Louisiana would rather not spend the whole summer on an island with her grandparents, but that's before she meets George. This quiet book speaks volumes about building your life and the support system that sustains it.

SAM MILLER,
Carmichael's Bookstore

☐ *Dear Sister*
by Alison McGhee,
ill. by Joe Bluhm / ages 10–12

This sweet, heartfelt, and funny graphic novel is a tribute to the slow starting, initially reluctant relationship that is sibling love. Its spot-on art and message will resonate with adults and children.

SAM MILLER,
Carmichael's Bookstore

BOOKS ABOUT
friendship

Who is a true friend? These books show readers that even the most unlikely pairs can overcome challenges, be there for each other, and have wonderful adventures together.

☐ *Stay*
**by Kate Klise,
ill. by M. Sarah Klise / ages 3–8**

Astrid realizes that her dog, Eli, is getting older, so she makes a bucket list of experiences they can share together. A beautiful look at the relationship between a child and pet that celebrates making loving memories.

**BREIN LOPEZ,
Children's Book World**

☐ *The Scarecrow*
**by Beth Ferry,
ill. by the Fan Brothers / ages 4–6**

A scary scarecrow steps out of his comfort zone to rescue a baby crow. Despite their differences, they form a special friendship that lasts through the seasons.

**RAE ANN PARKER,
Parnassus Books**

☐ *Stormy*
by Guojing / ages 3–7

This powerful, wordless story is both touching and compelling. Supported by magical artwork, you provide the narrative about a puppy discovered under a bench.

**SARAH YEWMAN,
picture books blogger**

☐ *George and Martha*
by James Marshall / ages 4–7

Just like human friends, George and Martha are fallible, occasionally troublesome, and always hilarious. Whether spying on each other, losing a tooth, or having a picnic, these two pals are truly tons of fun.

**EMMA STRAUB,
Books Are Magic**

☐ Little Bear's Friend
by Else Holmelund Minarik,
ill. by Maurice Sendak / ages 4–7

The forest is filled with friends and adventure in this beginning chapter book. When one friend moves away, Little Bear must learn to deal with loss. Thankfully he finds a way to keep in touch!

**ANGIE MURCHISON TALLY,
the Country Bookshop**

☐ The Doll People
by Ann M. Martin and Laura Godwin,
ill. by Brian Selznick / ages 8–12

When a new plastic family moves into the dollhouse next to the respected porcelain family, no one thinks they will have anything in common. Then Auntie Sarah goes missing, and the two families need to work together!

**ANGIE MURCHISON TALLY,
the Country Bookshop**

☐ Bearnard's Book
by Deborah Underwood,
ill. by Misa Saburi / ages 4–8

Bearnard is going to be in a book! But what will his book be about? Bearnard's friend Gertie helps him prepare for his book by encouraging Bearnard and calming his nerves.

**AMANDA MALDONADO,
Carmichael's Bookstore**

☐ Hurricane Child
by Kacen Callender / ages 8–12

Caroline deals with a lot— her mom leaving, bullies at school, and the possibility of a "ghost" who keeps following her. Then her new best friend Kalinda moves to the island and helps Caroline weather her problems.

**SARA WIGGLESWORTH,
Green Apple Books**

☐ Brave
by Svetlana Chmakova / ages 5 & up

Jensen is one of the best heroes ever! He's not "cool" or physically strong, but he stays true to himself while he learns the value of real friendship.

**SARA WIGGLESWORTH,
Green Apple Books**

Add your own favorites:

_____

_____

_____

BOOKS ABOUT
people who make a difference

With stories of real people who broke barriers, or fictional characters who stand up for what they believe in, these books will start conversations about how to create change in the world.

Add your own favorites:

_____

_____

_____

☐ *An ABC of Equality*
by Chana Ginelle Ewing,
ill. by Paulina Morgan / ages 4–6

An introduction to social justice with lessons from ability to immigration. Each word is accompanied by a two-sentence simplified definition that explains the impact of these concepts in ways children can understand.

VERA AHIYYA,
the Tutu Teacher

☐ *The Important Thing About Margaret Wise Brown*
by Mac Barnett,
ill. by Sarah Jacoby / ages 4–8

A biography of the legendary children's book author of *Goodnight Moon*. At the heart of this book, Barnett reminds us that not all books are for all kids, and that is OK.

CATHY BERNER,
Blue Willow Bookshop

☐ *It Began with a Page: How Gyo Fujikawa Drew the Way*
by Kyo Maclear,
ill. by Julie Morstad / ages 4–8

This is the biography of a Japanese American artist who was determined to portray racial diversity in her picture books, and prevailed with her bestseller, *Babies*.

KELLIE DIGUANGCO,
Secret Society of Books

☐ *At the Mountain's Base*
by Traci Sorell,
ill. by Weshoyot Alvitre / ages 4–8

The beautiful story of Millie Rexroat, the only Native American woman to serve in the WWII Women Airforce Service Pilots. This story portrays hope, family, and pride.

VERA AHIYYA,
the Tutu Teacher

☐ *The Youngest Marcher*
by Cynthia Levinson,
ill. by Vanessa Brantley-Newton / ages 5–10

Nine-year-old Audrey was the youngest marcher to take to the streets and be sent to jail for marching for civil rights. Use this story to encourage children to speak up for what they believe is right.

MAYA LE ESPIRITU,
MaiStoryBook

☐ *Planting Stories: The Life of Librarian and Storyteller Pura Belpré*
by Anika Aldamuy Denise,
ill. by Paola Escobar / ages 4–8

Engaging illustrations and text share the inspiring story of Pura Belpré, who enriched children's literature with her enchanting Puerto Rican folktales.

ROSEMARY D'URSO,
LibraryMom.com

☐ *Breakout*
by Kate Messner / ages 9–14

When two inmates from the local prison escape, Nora, Lizzie, and Elidee see a different side of their community—one of fear, ignorance, and societal racism. Their desire to change it will linger with readers.

SARA WIGGLESWORTH,
Green Apple Books

☐ *Mary Wears What She Wants*
by Keith Negley / ages 4–8

This picture book is inspired by the true story of Mary Edwards Walker. When Mary was young, little girls only wore skirts. Mary decides she wants to wear something that makes playing easier—pants!

AMANDA MALDONADO,
Carmichael's Bookstore

☐ *Midnight Without a Moon*
by Linda Williams Jackson / ages 10–12

Thirteen-year-old Rose Lee Carter strives to make a difference in her 1955 Mississippi hometown after fourteen-year-old Emmett Till is killed for allegedly whistling at a white woman in the next town over.

RAE ANN PARKER,
Parnassus Books

BOOKS FOR
bedtime

Settle into bed with a story that will calm even the most rambunctious child. These sleepy tales will put your little one right to sleep after a little bit of sweet snuggle time.

☐ *Go to Sleep, Little Farm*
by Mary Lyn Ray,
ill. by Christopher Silas Neal /
ages 0–3

A quiet, peaceful journey around the farm as all the creatures tuck in for the night. Rhyming text and lovely illustrations make for a cozy read. Perfect for a cuddle.

JESSI BLACKSTOCK,
Magers & Quinn Booksellers

☐ *Good Night Owl*
by Greg Pizzoli / ages 3–5

A friendship story with a twist. Owl is settled into bed when he hears a strange noise. He searches and searches, not noticing the little mouse keeping him awake.

RAE ANN PARKER,
Parnassus Books

☐ *Ten, Nine, Eight*
by Molly Bang / ages 0–3

Ten small toes and nine soft friends invite the youngest listeners to settle down for bed in this sweet, simple, Caldecott Honor–winning book that is just perfect for cuddling before bedtime.

ANGIE MURCHISON TALLY,
the Country Bookshop

☐ *Mr. Pumpkin's Tea Party*
by Erin Barker / ages 3–5

Learn your numbers while attending the dream-worthy tea party of Mr. Pumpkin and his friends in this charmingly quiet counting picture book.

NICOLE BRINKLEY,
Oblong Books & Music

☐ *Little Penguins*
by Cynthia Rylant,
ill. by Christian Robinson / ages 3–7

A family of young penguins excitedly watch the snowfall. They put on scarves, mittens, socks, and boots and head outside. Lovely prose and illustrations create a bedtime story for all to enjoy.

CATHY BERNER,
Blue Willow Bookshop

☐ *If I Was the Sunshine*
by Julie Fogliano,
ill. by Loren Long / ages 4–8

This sweet picture book explores love and connections in unique ways with lyrical text and beautiful illustrations. A quiet book perfect for reading and rereading.

RAE ANN PARKER,
Parnassus Books

☐ *Time for Bed, Miyuki*
by Roxane Marie Galliez,
ill. by Seng Soun Ratanavanh /
ages 3–7

A beautiful book depicting how imagination comes to life right before bedtime. The illustrations are dreamy and lovely.

SARA WIGGLESWORTH,
Green Apple Books

☐ *Stop That Yawn*
by Caron Levis,
ill. by LeUyen Pham / ages 5–8

This enchanting bedtime story stars an exuberant main character who tries to avoid going to sleep. The countless mentions of yawning, however, will relax readers and help them succumb to their own sleepiness.

ROSEMARY D'URSO,
LibraryMom.com

☐ *Home*
by Carson Ellis / ages 4–8

This book pairs dreamy art with simple words. It is a comforting notion that home can look a lot of different ways. As long as it's full of the people that matter to you, home is perfect just the way it is.

EMMA STRAUB,
Books Are Magic

Add your own favorites:

_____

_____

_____

Sincere gratitude to all of the contributors to this book:

Abby Rauscher, Amanda Maldonado, Angie Murchison Tally, Brein Lopez, Cathy Berner, Christine Utz, Damita Nocton, Emma Straub, Jessi Blackstock, Kellie Diguangco, Lauren Savage, Maya Le Espiritu, Melissa Posten, Nicole Brinkley, Rae Ann Parker, Rosemary D'Urso, Sam Miller, Sara Wigglesworth, Sarah Yewman, Susan Straub, and Vera Ahiyya

Editor: Karrie Witkin
Designer: Diane Shaw
Production Manager: Rebecca Westall

ISBN: 978-1-4197-4140-1

Foreword © 2021 Emma Straub
Text © 2021 Abrams

Cover © 2021 Abrams

Published in 2021 by Abrams Image, an imprint of ABRAMS. All rights reserved. No portion of this book may be reproduced, stored in a retrieval system, or transmitted in any form or by any means, mechanical, electronic, photocopying, recording, or otherwise, without written permission from the publisher.

Printed and bound in China
10 9 8 7 6 5 4 3 2 1

Abrams Image books are available at special discounts when purchased in quantity for premiums and promotions as well as fundraising or educational use. Special editions can also be created to specification. For details, contact specialsales@abramsbooks.com or the address below.

Abrams Image® is a registered trademark of Harry N. Abrams, Inc.

ABRAMS The Art of Books
195 Broadway, New York, NY 10007
abramsbooks.com

MIX
Paper from
responsible sources
FSC® C144853